PLANT-TASTIC!
GOTCHA!

MEAT-EATING PLANTS

BY REX RUBY

Minneapolis, Minnesota

Credits

Cover and title page, © Lezh/iStock, © malerapaso/iStock, © Oksana Akhtanina/iStock, and © Cathy Keifer/Shutterstock; Design elements used throughout, © eNJoy Istyle/Adobe Stock; 4, © Alekss/Adobe Stock and © Rybnikova Olga/Shutterstock; 4–5, © marcouliana/iStock; 6, © Recebin/iStock; 7, © Okea/Adobe Stock and © rangizzz/Shutterstock; 8–9, © Carol Dembinsky/Dembinsky Photo Associates/Alamy and © blickwinkel/Hecker/Alamy; 10–11, © corlaffra/Adobe Stock; 12, © Ed Reschke/Getty Images; 13, © AY Images/Alamy; 14, © Andreas Häuslbetz/iStock; 14–15, © Jaroslav Moravcik/Shutterstock; 16–17, © SERGEY ALESHIN/iStock; 18, © wildcat78/iStock; 19, © Catherine Brown/Alamy; 20, © Muhammad Arie/iStock; 20–21, © Margarita Borge Santiago/Shutterstock; 22 Step 1–2, © ILYA AKINSHIN/Adobe Stock; 22 Step 3, © 1981 Rustic Studio/Adobe Stock and © korkeng/Adobe Stock; 22 Step 4, © KateLeigh/iStock; and 23, © piyaset/iStock, © Masummerbreak/iStock, and © Dewin ' Indew/iStock.

Bearport Publishing Company Product Development Team

President: Jen Jenson; Director of Product Development: Spencer Brinker; Managing Editor: Allison Juda; Associate Editor: Naomi Reich; Senior Designer: Colin O'Dea; Associate Designer: Elena Klinkner; Associate Designer: Kayla Eggert; Product Development Specialist: Anita Stasson

Library of Congress Cataloging-in-Publication Data

Names: Ruby, Rex, author.
Title: Gotcha! : meat-eating plants / by Rex Ruby.
Other titles: Meat-eating plants |
Description: Minneapolis, Minnesota : Bearport Publishing Company, [2024] |
  Series: Plant-tastic! | Includes bibliographical references and index.
Identifiers: LCCN 2022058252 (print) | LCCN 2022058253 (ebook) | ISBN
  9798888220405 (hardcover) | ISBN 9798888222331 (paperback) | ISBN
  9798888223550 (ebook)
Subjects: LCSH: Carnivorous plants--Juvenile literature.
Classification: LCC QK917 .R83 2024 (print) | LCC QK917 (ebook) | DDC |
  583/.887--dc23/eng/20221216
LC record available at https://lccn.loc.gov/2022058252
LC ebook record available at https://lccn.loc.gov/2022058253

Copyright © 2024 Bearport Publishing Company. All rights reserved. No part of this publication may be reproduced in whole or in part, stored in any retrieval system, or transmitted in any form or by any means, electronic, mechanical, photocopying, recording, or otherwise, without written permission from the publisher.

For more information, write to Bearport Publishing, 5357 Penn Avenue South, Minneapolis, MN 55419.

CONTENTS

Trapped! 4

A Sunny Snack. 6

Meat-Eating Plants. 8

Insects Beware! 10

Yummy Soup 12

Goodbye, Fly!. 14

A Sticky End 16

A Watery Trap 18

Tricky Plants 20

Science Lab. 22

Glossary. 23

Index 24

Read More. 24

Learn More Online. 24

About the Author. 24

TRAPPED!

A buzzing fly lands on the leaf of a small plant. The **insect** doesn't know it, but it has just made a big mistake. The plant is a Venus flytrap. Suddenly, the leaves snap shut! The fly is now the plant's prisoner, and there is no escape. This plant eats meat!

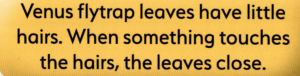

Venus flytrap leaves have little hairs. When something touches the hairs, the leaves close.

A SUNNY SNACK

Most plants get their **energy** through **photosynthesis** (*foh*-toh-SIN-thi-sis). First, they pull water from the ground and **carbon dioxide** from the air. Then, they use sunlight to turn the water and gas into food. Plants can also take in **nutrients** from the soil they are growing in.

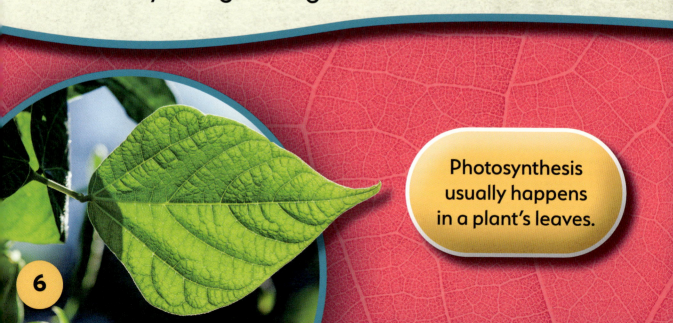

Photosynthesis usually happens in a plant's leaves.

MEAT-EATING PLANTS

For some plants, the sun and soil just aren't enough. Plants that grow where soil has few nutrients have a different way to get their energy. They get what they need from living things. These meat-eaters chow down on insects, spiders, and even small animals.

Meat-eating plants can be found on every **continent** except Antarctica.

The butterwort plant eats mosquitoes, flies, and other flying insects.

INSECTS BEWARE!

Many meat-eating plants look and smell nice. They are made to attract a meal with bright colors and sweet nectar. But when **prey** gets too close, it is in for a surprise. It may get stuck on gluey leaves. A plant may snap shut, trapping the bug in a cage. Sometimes, prey even drowns to death.

There are many types of meat-eating plants. They have different kinds of traps.

YUMMY SOUP

Once they have caught their meal, the plants ooze juices that break down the soft parts of flesh. Then, they soak up the nutrients from the soup they've made. *Yum!* Most meat-eating plants suck in their meals over about five days, but it can take nearly two months for others to finish the food.

The nutrient **nitrogen** helps meat-eating plants grow their leaves.

GOODBYE, FLY!

The Venus flytrap is one of the only plants that moves to catch its prey. When a fly walks across its open leaves, the plant closes a leafy trap. After it has finished eating, the trap opens again. All that's left of the fly is a dry shell!

The Venus flytrap closes only if it has felt something touch it multiple times in a row.

A STICKY END

The sundew plant uses a gluey nectar to catch insects. Its leaves are covered in long **tentacles**. The tip of each tentacle is tacky. When an insect lands on the plant, it becomes stuck. Then, the sundew's leaf slowly curls around the bug and covers it with more tentacles.

What happens if a sundew catches something that isn't food? The leaf uncurls to release it.

A trapped insect

A WATERY TRAP

Some meat-eating plants drown their prey. The pitcher plant has a long tube that holds liquid in the bottom. If a bug walks along the slippery edge of the tube, it falls in. The smooth inside of the trap stops any prey from climbing out. The meaty meal eventually drowns.

Bugs aren't the only food for pitcher plants. Sometimes, rats and lizards fall into their traps, too!

A trapped lizard

TRICKY PLANTS

From sticky glue to slippery tubes—these plants have many ways to catch their next meal. And once prey is caught in one of these tricky traps, there's no way to avoid turning into a yummy soup. What will these green killers snatch up next?

Some people grow meat-eating plants at home. They even hand-feed their plants insects!

SCIENCE LAB
BE A PLANT SCIENTIST

Most plants get some nutrients from the soil. Find out which soil is better for growing seeds.

1. Add soil from your garden or yard to a pot.

2. Put potting soil in another pot. Label each container.

3. Plant two bean seeds in each container. In a notebook, write down which plants you think will grow better and why.

4. Put the containers in a sunny spot and water them regularly. As they start to grow, write down which plant grows faster. Which looks healthier?

GLOSSARY

carbon dioxide a gas people and animals breathe out that plants need to survive

continent one of the world's seven large land masses

energy the power needed by all living things to grow and stay alive

insect a small animal that has six legs, three main body parts, and a hard covering

nitrogen a nutrient that living things need to grow

nutrients substances plants and animals need to grow and stay healthy

photosynthesis the process plants use to make food from water, carbon dioxide, and sunlight

prey an animal that is eaten by another living thing

tentacles long, thin parts of some plants and animals

INDEX

carbon dioxide 6
drown 10, 18
food 6, 16, 18
glue 10, 16, 20
leaves 4, 6–7, 9–10, 12, 14, 16
nectar 10–11, 16
nutrients 6, 8, 12, 22
photosynthesis 6
pitcher plant 18
soil 6, 8, 22
sundew plant 16
Venus flytraps 4, 14–15

READ MORE

Claybourne, Anna. *How Can a Plant Eat a Fly? and Other Questions about Plants (A Question of Science).* New York: Crabtree Publishing Company, 2021.

Davies, Monika. *Plants Can Eat Meat! (Plants with Superpowers).* New York: Gareth Stevens, 2023.

Griffin, Mary. *Carnivorous Pitcher Plants (Fantastic Plants).* New York: PowerKids Press, 2023.

LEARN MORE ONLINE

1. Go to **www.factsurfer.com** or scan the QR code below.
2. Enter "**Gotcha**" into the search box.
3. Click on the cover of this book to see a list of websites.

ABOUT THE AUTHOR

Rex Ruby lives in Minnesota with his family. He's glad he's too big to get stuck in a meat-eating plant.